THE LITTLE BOOK OF

HOPE

PAUL WILSON

PENGUIN BOOKS

PENGUIN BOOKS

Published by the Penguin Group
Penguin Books Ltd, 27 Wrights Lane, London W8 5TZ, England
Penguin Putnam Inc., 375 Hudson Street, New York, New York 10014, USA
Penguin Books Australia Ltd, Ringwood, Victoria, Australia
Penguin Books Canada Ltd, 10 Alcorn Avenue, Toronto, Ontario, Canada M4V 3B2
Penguin Books (NZ) Ltd, Private Bag 102902, NSMC, Auckland, New Zealand

Penguin Books Ltd, Registered Offices: Harmondsworth, Middlesex, England

Published in Great Britain by Penguin Books 1999
10 9 8 7 6 5 4 3 2

Copyright © The Calm Centre Pty Ltd, 1999
All rights reserved

Set in Monotype Phaistos
Typeset by Midland Typesetters, Maryborough, Victoria
Printed in England by William Clowes Ltd

Remember when life was filled with wonder? When you looked forward to the next morning with excitement and anticipation? When every new day promised an adventure that you could hardly wait to get involved in?

You can bring back that feeling again.

The Little Book of Hope was created to add a sprinkling of hope and optimism to your day.

Let this book fall open to any page for the suggestion that will work best for you at this moment. Accept it at face value. Let your subconscious have its way.

And, if you allow it to happen, the days ahead will continue to look better and better.

Conquer all workplace tensions with
Paul Wilson's complete work,
Calm at Work.

'His jargon-free, no-nonsense ideas
are remarkably simple.'
Evening Standard

YOU HAVE TO ADMIT IT'S GETTING BETTER

While today's media try to convince us that the world is shedding goodness and opportunity every day, the opposite is the case.

Globally speaking, life is getting better all the time – the average person is healthier, more prosperous, free and aware, with significantly better prospects than ever before.

Enjoy it.

WHILE YOU HAVE BREATH, YOU HAVE HOPE

When you no longer worry about the future, and no longer have regrets about the past, you exist purely in the moment. If you concentrate on that moment you instinctively know that as long as you have life you have hope.

Enjoy the moment. Breathe easily. Relax.

Now you're feeling happy

Happiness is not something you have to deserve or work for; indeed, the more you pursue it, the more elusive it becomes. Happiness is here for the accepting now.

Be prepared to accept it – now – and you will have so much more to look forward to.

HOPE HEALS

One of the discoveries of modern
medicine is that the more optimistic you
are, the greater your chances of
maintaining or improving health.

Indeed many prominent specialists insist
that the greatest indicator of wellness
and longevity is the simple belief
that you will be well and will live a
long time.

BE OPTIMISTIC ABOUT YOUR SUCCESS

It is one of life's truisms that most optimists succeed in life. It is also a truism that *all* pessimists fail.

By any measure, then, there's a lot to be gained from working on your optimism.

HANG OUT WITH THE HOPEFUL

A sure way of achieving what you want in life is to mix with those who have already achieved it. Make friends with those who are heading in the direction you wish to head, and be wary of those heading elsewhere.

Make friends with the optimistic and hopeful.

HOPE INTO ACTION

Some people believe hope is nothing
more than an expectation of certain
outcomes.

It is more than this. Hope is a real
commitment to positive behaviour and
attitudes. In other words, hope is active,
not passive.

Make this commitment and life
starts to look rosier.

RELAX

A tense frame of mind invariably encourages a negative perspective. And the more you succumb to the tensions of the day, the bleaker this perspective appears.

A calm state of mind is usually accompanied by hope and optimism. Maintain the calm, and you maintain the hope.

THE OLDER WE GET, THE MORE THEY NEED US

The belief that you become less useful as you age is fast becoming outdated.

As the world population continues to age, at some time in the next decade or so older employees will be more in demand, and will be able to command higher wages, than their younger counterparts.

The best is yet to come!

IMAGINE THE GREAT TIMES AHEAD

Your subconscious has such power that whatever you can imagine, it will help you make a reality. Whatever you dream of, start it now.

Merely embarking on that course has a power and magic you may never have dreamed possible.

BE ENTHUSIASTIC ABOUT TOMORROW

There is no more effective or contagious force than enthusiasm. It helps you to achieve the 'impossible', it encourages others to share your optimism, and it guarantees that the future holds promise.

Be enthusiastic!

THE LONGER YOU WAIT, THE LONGER YOU GET

One of the delightful discoveries of growing older is the realisation that, statistically speaking, the older you get, the more your life expectancy increases.

Moreover, your life expectancy has been growing each year; it has lengthened by two years over the past decade.

All these extra years to get what you desire out of life!

ENCOURAGE GREA

Whatever your role, you have within yourself the ability to encourage and inspire others to achieve greater things.

There is a dual benefit to this.

The first is that someone else will go on to achieve something of worth. The second is that you will be encouraged and inspired yourself.

BE THANKFUL FOR TODAY

If you had been born in earlier times,
you would have hoped that things would
be better in the future.

And they are! You live longer, enjoy
more rights, and suffer less from
debilitating illnesses. And, most
importantly, you are more likely than
ever before to see your children
grow to maturity.

DOUBLE THE PLEASURE

In doing good for others, you derive a
dual benefit.

First, any act of altruism is its own
reward, because selfless acts help you to
feel hopeful and optimistic. Second, the
memories that induce the most positive
feelings are invariably of things done out
of love or generosity.

*Dream as if you'll live forever. Live as if
you'll die today.*

JAMES DEAN

SEE WHAT NO-ONE ELSE HAS MADE

It is worth looking closely at anything not man-made — the curve of a mountain, the flow of a stream, or the endlessness of the heavens.

This will reveal not only the splendour of the creator, but the peace and contentment of the viewer.

It may also reveal that you are not alone in the world.

*We are each of us angels with only one
wing; and we can only fly by embracing one
another.*

LUCIANO DE CRESCENZO

WEAR ROSE-COLOURED GLASSES

There are many prominent doomsayers who say that to see only the good in life is to ignore reality.

If reality means seeing more of the negative side of life, then you will profit from changing your reality. You can do that easily by searching for the good and going out of your way to find it.

THE PHYSICAL SIDE OF HOPE

One of the often overlooked advantages
of looking after your physical health
– with regular exercise and healthy diet –
is the way it enhances your feelings
about yourself and your future.

Look after your physical body and your
future will take care of itself.

Hope is the only good that is common to all men; those who have nothing else possess hope still.

THALES OF MILETUS

A SOLUTION IS AT HAND

The pessimists tell us that our planet is
being ravaged and the end is nigh.

Yet this is clearly not so.

If you look, there are simple,
long-term solutions to water, food
and energy shortages.

If you look for the good side,
it's there to be found.

Enjoy the First-time Experience

Try this simple exercise and the
wonder of life will reveal itself:
every sight you see, every sound you
hear, every taste you taste, imagine
you are experiencing it for the very
first time.

Or the last.

You can't help but be encouraged by
the result.

CELEBRATE YOUR BIRTHDAY

When your birthday arrives you have a
choice: you can moan about growing
older, or you can celebrate the
miraculous achievement that your life
has been to date.

If there's one thing about your existence
worth celebrating, it's an achievement
like being alive.

TAKE UP THE CHALLENGE

When you strive to improve yourself
and your world, you infuse your life
with purpose. Not only does this add
hope and satisfaction to your days, but it
overcomes boredom as well.

And, if what you strive for is central to
your fundamental needs and values, your
life begins to look even rosier still.

FORGET THE GOOD OLD DAYS

Nostalgia-lovers have always
romanticised 'the good old days'.

If romanticising this way makes you feel
good, fine. But if it makes you look less
favourably on today, remember this:
nostalgia colours the past so that only
its better features are recalled.

All opportunity and positive
possibilities exist in the future.

SEEK OUT THE POSITIVE

No doubt you have heard the maxim that
you can achieve what you put your
mind to.

This applies equally to negative thoughts
as to positive.

So if you're going to focus on anything,
it might as well be the positive things in
life you want to achieve.

TRY THE OTHER PATH

If you conclude that you've been heading
down the wrong path in your journey
through life, and despair because you've
waited so long to change direction,
consider this: a different path means a
fresh start, with no baggage, and with
the potential of something magical
waiting for you — somewhere just
around the next corner.

YOU HAVE WHAT IT TAKES

Very little is needed to create a happy,
hopeful life for yourself. It is contained
in your way of thinking.

Happiness, contentedness and hope all
depend on the content of your thoughts.
Dwell on the positive and the hopeful,
and you'll find you have all you need
to realise these qualities.

IS IT NORMAL TO BE HOPEFUL?

Some psychologists believe depression is created when we compare ourselves with others: we feel good when we measure up well, when we conform to or exceed the norm; we feel bad when we do not.

Norms are dangerous measures.

Accept your own uniqueness and most of these pressures vanish.

DECIDE TO BE HOPEFUL

Abraham Lincoln said that a man is about as happy as he makes up his mind to be.

So, too, with hope: you're about as hopeful as you make up your mind to be. And your future has about as much to offer as you make up your mind to allow it to have.

WAIT TWENTY YEARS

How much better and more fulfilling
could your life be if you had all of your
life to get it right?

Guess what: you do!

The only limit to what you can achieve
is the decision you make now. Go on,
decide to create an extraordinary future.
You have all the time in the world left
to create it.

He who has health has hope; and he who has hope, has everything.

PROVERB

EVERYTHING IS POSSIBLE

Since the advent of quantum mechanics, scientists have been telling us that few things are as they appear, and nothing is certain.

Think of the extraordinary possibilities this presents: when nothing is certain, everything is possible!

It is never too late to be what you might have been.

GEORGE ELIOT

LOOK FORWARD TO AN INTERESTING ANECDOTE

How often have you noticed that today's biggest worry turns out to be tomorrow's most interesting anecdote?

Generally, the problems of the day become less threatening with the passage of time. If you imagine yourself at some time in the future, looking back on your worries of today, you will discover they are lessened substantially.

ALTER YOUR IMMEDIATE WORLD

If you express yourself positively within your immediate surroundings, you help yourself to feel happier and more fulfilled.

Make the effort to make your immediate environment more appealing – with music, greenery, pets, décor, flowers, essential oils – and life will be more appealing as a result.

Be the change that you want to see in the world.

GANDHI

TOMORROW IS A BLANK PAGE

Some people choose to see their future as a story already written — not necessarily by their own hand.

Others see their future as a blank sheet just waiting for that magic touch to be added. With the prospect of a page this clean, aren't you excited about the creative possibilities?

CARRY A NOTEBOOK

Every day you encounter dozens of
thoughts and experiences that give you
hope, satisfaction and reason for living.
Then, all too often, you forget them at
the first sign of a setback.

Carry a notebook. Write them down.
You'll have a record of your inspiration
that you can refer to in times of need.

One joy dispels a hundred cares.

CONFUCIUS

PERSIST

There is one characteristic that promises
more positive results than both
knowledge and natural talent, and is
more reliable than luck.

Persistence.

If you just keep on going, maintaining
your hope and belief that something good
will happen, it generally does.

SAVOUR EVERY MORSEL

If you were told that the lunch before you was your very last meal, you'd be sure to savour every bite.

Every meal is an experience, and every taste is unique, so you might as well take your time and enjoy it.

Remind yourself often to apply this principle to all experiences in life.

LEARN NEW TRICKS

It's never too late to change.

The difference between being a slave to
habit and feeling in control of your life
is nothing more than the operation of a
tiny electrical circuit in your brain.

Change your perspective, and you
alter this circuit. All it takes
is commitment.

YOU HAVE CHOICES

As long as you are alive, you have
choices.

Sometimes they may be difficult to see,
or it may take a little creativity to
identify them, but they are always
waiting to be found.

Be on the lookout for them. Relish them.
Make the most of them.

LOOK FORWARD WITH HOPE

Maybe it is possible to imagine a time
when life can get no worse.

But take comfort, as it is *impossible*
to imagine a time when life cannot
get better.

This means there is always something
positive to look forward to.

CHANGE FOR THE BETTER

When you focus on growth being
adventurous and enriching, as opposed
to threatening, you can't help but thrive.

The moment you decide to welcome
change, and the untold good it can bring,
you discover that you always have
something to look forward to.

THE ART OF HOPE

Adding hope to our lives has long been the role of the artist — the painter, poet, musician, composer, actor, and author.

Today you have direct access to more collected art, literature, musical compositions and new artistic mediums, than existed in the entire world only a century ago.

DREAM ON

Regardless of your age, position or state
of health you are completely unfettered
in the dreams that you can have.

Not only are they infinitely extendable –
full of untapped possibilities and beauty
– but they're infinitely renewable as
well. And in your dreams, you can be as
daring as you dare.

ENJOY YOURSELF

The most satisfying way to add hope
and harmony to your life is to enjoy it
to the fullest.

When you do this, you make the world a
more agreeable place for yourself. You
also make it more agreeable for others —
enjoyment can be every bit as contagious
as optimism.

TAKE A LESSON FROM RABBITS

When life gets you down, and all the traumas and tragedies of civilisation seem overwhelming, go somewhere quiet where you can watch animals at play.

See how they accept life as it is . . . playing, being, living in the moment?

Try it for yourself. You don't have to be wild to enjoy it.

MOVE ON

There will be times when aspects of
your life appear to run off the rails.
Mistakes, calamities, transgressions. But
the beauty of life is that there is always
another chance; you can make a fresh
start any moment you choose.

As Mary Pickford once said, 'This thing
we call failure is not the falling down,
but the staying down'.

CONCENTRATE ON THE GOOD TIMES

Miserable people get the same number of good-time opportunities as happy people.

But miserable people tend to overlook this.

If you see only the miserable things, chances are you'll end up miserable. But if you look for the good times ahead, and reflect on those past, you'll feel much more hopeful.

THE EVIDENCE OF LIFE IS GROWTH

It is a curious characteristic of human beings that we try to cling to the things we have — even if they bring us no happiness or are not the things we particularly want.

Yet the real evidence of life is growth. Only by accepting change can you grow.

EXERCISE YOUR OPTIMISM

You are well aware of all the wonderful benefits that exercise brings to your body and your overall state of health.

Just as important is what it does for your spirit.

Exercise regularly and you'll feel more optimistic, with a more hopeful outlook on life. Isn't that worth getting in a sweat over?

TURN TO THE SUN

Have you ever noticed that the most melancholy moments of your day seem to occur indoors, at night?

The wonder of sunshine is that it injects hopefulness and optimism into your day. It works this way for almost all human beings.

If it's overcast, use your imagination and pretend.

TAKE THE GOOD
WITH THE BAD

Few things in life are inherently good or bad: they change according to when they occur, who is viewing them, and how they are viewed. Realising this can be the key to finding hope in even the most difficult situations.

Often you will find it productive to try to see another perspective on events in your life.

HAVE HUNDRED-YEAR GOALS

An inspiring characteristic of today's centenarians is that most of them claim to still have goals and ambitions.

It is vital to have goals and ambitions — even little ones. This will keep you youthful and hopeful.

SOMETHING TO FEEL POSITIVE ABOUT

Cynics say that all the positive attitude in the world won't help you succeed where you would normally fail.

But they miss the point: a positive attitude is its own reward. It improves health, overcomes sadness, and generally makes you feel good about life.

Any way you look at it, that's positive.

TELL YOURSELF THERE'S HOPE

When you tell yourself that there is so
much to live for, that life gets happier
and more fulfilling as it unfolds, you are
well on your way to discovering these
qualities for yourself.

Why? Because the words you use, like
the thoughts you have, powerfully
influence your beliefs.

BABYSIT

When they spend time with very young
children, most people are pleasantly
surprised to rediscover how much
potential the future has to offer.

What do children know that you have
forgotten? For a start, they know that
everything is possible.

Imagine how optimistic you'll feel when
you discover *this* again.

THE UNIVERSE DEPENDS ON YOU

No matter which way you look at it, the universe would not be the same without you. You play an integral role in its function.

Moreover, every day your contribution grows. Without making the slightest effort, you continue to make your mark.

On behalf of the rest of the universe, thank you for the role you play.

SOW A LITTLE HOPE

To watch something you've planted come to life does more than remind you of the splendour of nature.

It provides the most reassuring evidence that life continues: germinating, growing and eventually recycling itself – all done beautifully, seamlessly, and without fuss.

Maybe this is why gardening is the most popular hobby in the world.

PLAY THE GLAD GAME

Did you ever see the movie *Pollyanna*?

In it, Pollyanna plays a game where the aim is to find some aspect of every situation that she can be glad about.

Playing this game sometimes requires a little imagination, but the outcome is always the same: you feel better, and more hopeful, than before.

RISE TO HOPE

We sometimes feel a twinge of sadness when the sun goes down. We may also feel uplifted by the sunrise.

Maybe it's the sheer, uncomplicated beauty of the event. Or the inevitability of the day beginning again. Whatever it is, if you're up for the sunrise, you're guaranteed to feel youthful and alive.

TAKE THE AIR

For something so free and plentiful, it's extraordinary how many benefits flow from fresh air.

Foremost among these is the impact it has on your mood, the way you feel. Whether you find it in a park, in the country, by the beach, or in the mountains, seek out clean fresh air for feelings of optimism and hope.

MORE THAN HALF FULL

As you know, pessimists see a glass as half empty, where optimists see it as half full.

Even if the pessimists are right, you'll still end up with more than them if you view your glass through an optimist's eyes.

ASK YOUR DOG

If you want confirmation of how important and irreplaceable you are, check out the look on the face of your dog or cat next time you approach them.

Isn't it amazing how, even when you're at your most plain, your very existence excites them?

LOOK HOW WELL
YOU'RE DOING

If the amount of time you have to find
happiness and meaning in life is any
measure, you are living in the most
wonderful time in history.

In the Bronze Age you had only an
average of eighteen years, and in the
Middle Ages thirty-three years, to
discover these things. Today, you have
an average of seventy to eighty years.

GIVE THANKS FOR YOUR SETBACKS

Setbacks are seldom terminal. Indeed the size of the setbacks you have overcome is the best measure you have of your accomplishments to date.

Looking at it another way, Henry Ford once said: 'A setback is the opportunity to begin again more intelligently'.

CARRY CITRINE

The crystal citrine is said to cleanse the emotions and to promote happiness, inner strength and hope. Carry it with you to enhance these qualities.

LIVE POSITIVELY

As a predictor of longevity, a positive
attitude is so important that many
believe it has more bearing on your life
than any of the risk factors that are
conventionally cited – including
smoking, a sedentary lifestyle, diet
and genetics.

Look for the positive side of life,
and enjoy living longer.

MAKE EVERY NOTE COUNT

Some of the world's greatest musicians
say they play each performance as if it
were their last. You can hear the
difference; their passion cannot
be ignored.

Imagine the result if you played every
performance of your life this way.
How much more fulfilling and enjoyable
would it be?

SPREAD LOVE

Spread love everywhere you go . . . first of all in your own house. Give love to your children, to your wife or husband, to a next door neighbour . . . let no one ever come to you without leaving better and happier.

MOTHER TERESA

THINK OF A KISS

You can give your heart an inspiring
flutter with a single pleasant memory.

Recall that delicious moment when you
kissed someone — on impulse — and
suddenly realised that someone else
loved you as much as you loved them.

It's only a thought, but it still weaves
a magic.

GET OUT YOUR BABY PHOTOS

There was a time when every moment
was infused with hope
and wonder.

Recapture those feelings now using your
imagination. Simply bring out a photo of
yourself as a toddler, go somewhere
quiet and imagine what it was like then.

Bring that feeling of wonder back to
the present.

CELEBRATE YOUR FREEDOM

Most of the world's population enjoy a sense of personal freedom such as our ancestors could only fantasise about.

Make the most of this opportunity. Remind yourself, often, that the benefit of freedom is that it gives you choices. Moreover, you usually have more choices than may initially appear.

LEARN FROM THOSE LEARNING

They say the best teachers are those who learn from their students.

Simply observing a child learn something is one of the most hopeful experiences life has to offer.

Observe it. Encourage it. Learn from it.

YOU ARE NOT ALONE

One of the main causes of hopelessness,
we are told, is the feeling of isolation
that stems from loneliness.

To overcome this feeling, recognise that
you are not alone – there are countless
people about who would be grateful for
your company.

Be open to their arrival, and soon they
will appear.

SPRING AGAIN

Once you reach the darkest days of
winter, you notice that the sun is about
to shine again the moment you accept
spring is on the way.

No matter how joyless the winter, the
trees eventually spring back to life,
flowers bloom, and you cannot help but
feel young and vital.

What seems to us bitter trials are often
blessings in disguise.

OSCAR WILDE

PAUSE FOR A SMILE

In our busy, never-a-spare-moment world, we often lose sight of the fact that the simplest human reactions are often the most rewarding.

When you pause and smile at someone, communicating nothing more than your good feelings towards them, something powerful takes place – within you, and within them.

REMEMBER THE MAN IN RED

There was a time when your life had meaning and certainty. Then, you never stopped to question whether or not life was infused with hope.

To bring back that feeling now, recall those moments when you wrote letters to Santa Claus. Remember how hopeful you felt?

DREAM DURING THE DAY

Daydreams are inherently positive and hopeful. Participating in them has a positive and hopeful effect on the subconscious, which has a similar effect on the way you feel.

Daydream to your heart's content. It's positively good for you.

DO IT ON PURPOSE

When you have well-defined goals and purpose in life, you are much less affected by the obstacles that appear to stand in your way.

Obstacles are nothing more than what you see when your focus strays from your goals.

CHANGE FOR THE BETTER

All great achievements and successes in
life, and all changes for the better, have
one powerful characteristic in common:
the first step.

Take the first step, and the journey has a
way of taking care of itself.

REMOVE HAPPINESS FROM YOUR GOALS

Most people see happiness as a goal or objective in life. This is a sure way not to achieve it.

Happiness is not a goal, it is a process. It is a decision, a conscious choice for the present.

Decide to be happy – now – and the process has already begun.

SEE THE GOOD IN THE BAD

Although it sometimes takes effort and creativity to recognise this, there is good to be found in all misfortunes.

This is eloquently expressed in a phrase from Zen philosophy which translates as: 'Touch the hole in your life, and there the flowers will bloom'.

God grant me the courage to change the things I can, the patience to accept the things I can't, and the wisdom to know the difference.

THE SERENITY PRAYER

LOOK THE OTHER WAY

Whether you focus on the seedy and unpleasant, or on the positive and hopeful, your world will be defined by how you choose to look at it.

You can sidestep much of the unpleasantness of life simply by looking somewhere else. Concentrate on the beautiful.

IT GETS EASIER

You discovered this when you were learning to ride a bicycle, bake a cake or recite the alphabet: everything seems at its most difficult just before it starts to get easier.

So, relax. When things appear at their bleakest, your life is just about to take a turn for the better.

DO YOU SEE WHAT THEY SEE?

The difference between a problem and an
opportunity is attitude: losers see the
problem, whereas winners work at
seeing the opportunity.

Yes, they work at it.

Being able to see the opportunity rather
than the problem sometimes takes
persistence and discipline, but the
rewards are vast.

TAKE A DETOUR

We may feel at our most frustrated when a barrier stands in our way. But some of life's most fortuitous outcomes are the result of detours.

Welcome the detours. Often they redirect lives in a profitable way you may never have considered.

YOU DON'T HAVE TO BE A VICTIM

If you ever feel you are the victim of circumstance, consider this.

You can overcome this feeling with one simple action. The moment you go looking for, or trying to create, the circumstances you want, everything in life starts to fall into place.

PARADISE IS WHERE YOU ARE

Paradise is where I am.

VOLTAIRE

ASSUME

If you assume that there is hope for your
future, you guarantee there will be hope
for your future.

If only all things in life were as
uncomplicated as that.

THE POWER OF MANY THOUGHTS

You can think yourself into sadness or happiness, despair or hopefulness.

The easiest way to influence your way of thinking is not to try to manage each thought, but to manage the volume of one type of thought versus another. Create many hopeful thoughts, and guess how you'll be feeling.

Reflect upon your present blessings, of which every man has many; not on your past misfortunes, of which all men have some.

CHARLES DICKENS

WELCOME THE MISHAPS

There's a powerful old saying about the nature of mistakes – the person who makes no mistakes seldom makes anything.

Mishaps and mistakes are simply reminders that life is a creative process. And what lies ahead can be enhanced by experiencing what has gone before.

LOOK UP

One of the drawbacks of spending too
much time with downcast eyes is you
tend to miss one of life's most optimistic
symbols. The rainbow.

Usually this one image makes up for
having to stand in the rain.

FOLLOW YOUR NOSE

Certain scents – particularly some floral essential oils – stimulate the production of a neurochemical that helps you to feel optimistic.

Use your nose to determine the most effective of these: start with lavender, experiment with neroli and sandalwood, maybe add some pine or peppermint.

GO FORWARD

There are many things in life that you
simply cannot do anything about.
Foremost among these are things that
have already happened.

Even if you still bear the scars from it,
the past no longer exists – except as a
memory if you choose to recall it.
And even that memory fades if you
concentrate on now, and what lies ahead.

GO TO BED WITH
JANE AUSTEN

Jane Austen's *Pride and Prejudice* has become a classic for very good reason.

Take a copy to bed tonight. And, as you drift off, luxuriate in the hope and optimism that flow from her inspired pages.

AN END TO IGNORANCE

While some joke that ignorance is bliss, most believe that education is the key to establishing equality and enlightenment in this world.

Things are looking up. In just twenty years, global adult literacy has increased by more than fifty percent.

CUT YOURSELF SOME SLACK

We often add pressure to our day by aiming for artificial standards that we can never hope to meet.

Much can be said for having high standards, but you need a sense of being able to accomplish them. Sometimes this might mean relaxing them — just a little — so that they remain within reach.

RELAX

You may have experienced how stress and tension tend to suck the optimism out of life. But, fortunately, the converse is also true: hope and optimism seem to leap exuberantly from times of tranquillity.

Work at being calm, and hope will take care of itself.

HOPE FOR A FANTASY

We live in an age that celebrates the
rational and the pragmatic — neither
of which are qualities known for
inspiring hope.

When you occupy your mind with
fantasies and daydreams, you have it in
your power to nurture hope, and more
effectively than with any rational
thought you can imagine.

OPTIMISM FOR ITS OWN SAKE

While optimism may not be the one quality that makes the world go round, it certainly makes the ride worthwhile.

The harder you work at having an optimistic perspective, the more enjoyment you will derive from it.

TAKE THE COURSE OF GOOD HOPE

As any old salt will tell you, if you don't know what harbour you're heading for, no breeze will be the right breeze.

Same with the future. If you have no destination in mind, you won't know the right breezes when they come along.

Plan, relax, and go with the breeze.

*At the touch of love, everyone becomes
a poet.*

PLATO

YOU GET MANY CHANCES

One of the exciting by-products of a
maturing population is that you get
several shots at finding the career
you love.

It is now common for people to have
several different careers. A secretary
today and a scriptwriter tomorrow; a
dentist today, a diplomat tomorrow . . .

The only limit is your imagination.

IT'S NOT SO BLEAK AFTER ALL

When things look bleak and gloomy, you
have at least two things to look forward
to. First, morning always follows night.
Second, the longer you have to wait in
the darkness, the more you appreciate
the sheer wonder of the sunrise.

LOOK AT WHAT YOU HAVE

If your attention is on what you are
missing out on, you can be certain that
you will never have enough.

But if your attention is on what you
already have, you'll have more by
comparison.

CREATE A HOPEFUL FUTURE

Regardless of our skills or training, we all have a simple choice we can make in life – to be a consumer or a creator.

Being a creator is more satisfying and uplifting. What you create doesn't need to be brilliant, or even unique; it just needs to be made by you.

IT'S NOT WORTH WORRYING ABOUT

What we worry about seldom eventuates.

Worries exist only in the mind, and always relate to the future. Relaxed people tend to look at them in the same way they look at mud-puddles: messy today, but evaporated tomorrow.

HOPE IMPROVES YOUR GRADES

Studies have shown that one of the most powerful predictors of better exam results is not intelligence, commitment or grades. It's simply hoping for better results.

Not only is hope a powerful motivation, the greater the level of hope, the better the result.

KEEP YOUR EYE ON THE FUTURE

You limit your future when you concentrate on your past.

You can be so much more powerful and successful in the future. When you concentrate on this success – planning for it and envisioning yourself participating in it – you are well on your way to achieving it. It's only a matter of time.

Optimism is the faith that leads to achievement. Nothing can be done without hope and confidence.

HELEN KELLER

MAKE YOUR FACE HURT

Your simplest facial action — a smile —
happens when all your muscles relax,
which instantly makes you feel good,
emotionally and physically.

A laugh works even better. If you can
find nothing to laugh at, look harder.
If you still can't find anything, just laugh
for the hell of it.

ALL THAT 'DOING UNTO OTHERS'

For the past decade or so, there has been a resurgence of interest in religious or spiritual thinking.

As most of the major religions pay homage to variations on the Golden Rule (do unto others as you would have them do unto you), this can only be good news.

HOPE IN A BANANA SKIN

Aside from the obvious health benefits,
one of the interesting advantages of
foods high in potassium – such as
bananas – is that they encourage feelings
of wellbeing and cheerfulness.

Such a portable way to positively
influence the way you feel!

LOOK WHAT YOU CAN EXPECT

Expect nothing, but know that great
things lie ahead for you.

GIVE BIRTH

The arrival of a new baby is the embodiment of hope.

When you combine this event with a simple statistic – that a child born today has a better chance than ever before of prospering and remaining healthy until a ripe old age – that sense of hope increases even more.

COMMUNICATION IS EASIER

Some people despair when they feel
powerless to be heard or considered.

Yet never before in history have you had
such access to so many potential
listeners through communication
technology. And never before have
so many of these been so prepared to
listen to, and fight for the rights of,
the aggrieved.

THROW YOUR ARMS AROUND ANOTHER

There are studies that show regular hugs
not only increase feelings of
contentedness in life, but actually assist
in improving health and extending life
spans — for both givers and receivers.

There is no shortage of people who'd
love a hug.

BE THANKFUL YOU'RE
A WOMAN

The average girl born today can expect
to live around eighty years — time
enough to realise the most ambitious
of ambitions.

This life expectancy grows every year,
and has been doing so for the past
millennium.

BE THANKFUL YOU'RE A MAN

Although the life expectancy of the average man is slightly less than that of the average woman, there is still a major benefit in being male.

Women live longer because they tend to live longer with the diseases that men succumb to.

So even though a man's life is shorter, you could say it's sweeter.

GOOD NEWS FOR THE WORLD

According to the World Health Organisation the global population has never had a healthier outlook.

Life expectancy has increased more in the last fifty years than in the preceding 5000. Moreover, by 2025 the citizens of every nation on earth will enjoy a life expectancy of fifty or more years.

And it will get better yet.

TURN TO A FLOWER

Flower essences are a refined form of
herbal infusion. They restore balance
and encourage inner health and harmony.

Gentian, gorse and sweet chestnut are
just three of those said to counter
feelings of hopelessness and
discouragement, and to encourage
feelings of confidence and optimism.

*The beginning is the most important part of
the task.*

PLATO

HAVE A WORD TO YOURSELF

Try repeating these words to yourself —
a few times a day — quietly but
persuasively, as if you were trying to
convince somebody else of their
importance: 'Not only am I feeling good
now, I know there are even better times
ahead of me'.

Listen carefully to yourself saying it,
and you'll soon start to accept it.

LOOK FOR THE MAGIC

Every person who knows there is
wonder and magic in life is a person
who looked for it.

To discover the magic you have to be
looking for it — not only in the big
events, but in the smallest ones as well.

Cultivate this skill, and your life will
never be the same again.

TAKE HOPE FROM SCIENCE

There are hordes of eminent scientists
who believe that, in the next thirty
years, most of the world's major
diseases will have been overcome
through molecular biology
(gene therapy).

Even if we discount their optimism by
half, they've certainly given us a lot
to look forward to.

LET YOUR MIND WANDER

We daydream for a significant part of
our waking time, sometimes about the
past or the future, and at other times
about a fantasised present.

Daydreaming is an invaluable activity. It
offers your mind rest from time to time,
and is a place of unlimited hope.

TRUST THE STATISTICS

No matter how you analyse the statistics, if you take a global view of humanity you discover that the world is a pleasant place to live in, and that good usually prevails over evil.

If enough of us accept these statistics, think how much better the world will look.

THANK GOD FOR HONEST POLITICIANS

Today's politicians and public officials are more accountable than ever before.

Even though you may hear more about those who break the rules, it's the result of more media coverage — not more rule-breaking.

Doesn't it feel good to know our standards are at an all-time high?

There are only two ways to live your life:
one is as though nothing is a miracle;
the other is as if everything is.
I believe in the latter.

ALBERT EINSTEIN

It's all a matter of luck

One of life's injustices is that bad luck
usually befalls those who can least
afford it. Pessimists become accident-
prone . . . Bad luck comes in threes . . .

Yet the opposite also applies. When you
know where you're heading, and
optimistically concentrate on the path,
good fortune has a habit of coming along
with you.

All the great things are simple, and many can be expressed in a single word: freedom; justice; honour; duty; mercy; hope.

SIR WINSTON CHURCHILL

YOU HAVE THE POWER TO PROSPER

When it comes to health, the best predictor of survival we have is the simple question: How do you rate your health — excellent, very good, good, fair, poor?

This rating has a direct effect on your survival potential. It seems that people know things about themselves that doctors and scientists don't.

ACT AS IF THERE'S MUCH IN STORE

When you act as though life has so much more in store for you, you'll soon discover that it's true. Why? Because you convince your subconscious it's true, and this becomes self-fulfilling.

Try it — persuade everyone around you that you are enthusiastic about what lies ahead. You'll soon convince the most important person of all — yourself.

TURN WORDS INTO THOUGHTS

You talk to yourself most of the time;
this is known as internal dialogue. The
words you use in this play a major role
in the way you feel.

So why criticise or doubt yourself?
Congratulate yourself. Reassure
yourself, often. If there's one person it
pays to have on your side, it's you.

*If one advances confidently in the direction
of his dreams, and endeavors to live a life
which he has imagined, he will meet with a
success unexpected in common hours.*

HENRY DAVID THOREAU

THE GOOD OIL ON HOPE

Essential oils dispense pleasure while they work on your emotions.

Oils that are said to remove despondency and promote optimism include myrrh, orange, patchouli and bergamot.

A combination of two or more of these could work powerfully for you. Follow your nose to find the ideal combination.

MAKE NEW FRIENDS

Can you think of anything that inspires you and keeps you hopeful as much as the support of old friends?

Sometimes it is easy to overlook this simple understanding. Other times old friends need to be inspired, too. And never say no to the opportunity of making new friends.

TAKE PLEASURE IN AN EMPTY BOWL

There's an old Zen saying: 'Only an empty bowl can be filled'.

It means that the moment you think you have nothing left is the moment when growth and progress become inevitable.

Every time you see an empty bowl, think of the potential.

IT'S BEST WHEN YOU CAN'T

What's the best time to pause and relax
and reflect on all the good things you
have going for you?

On Sundays? In the evenings?

Possibly. But the very best times to
pause and relax are when you don't have
time to pause and relax. That's when a
pause has most benefit.

ANGER GIVES WAY TO LOVE

Of all the emotions, anger, love and
hope have most in common.

They're difficult to control, they
influence the way you perceive events,
and they are powerful motivations.

But that is the end of their similarities.
Anger diminishes feelings of hope,
while love arouses them.

YOU HAVE ALL THE TIME IN THE WORLD

Many believe that time pressure is the most prevalent stressor of the modern age.

But, when you think about it, you have the same amount of time at your disposal as there has ever been available. The only time you will ever have is this very moment. Make the most of it.

STARE INTO AN ARRANGEMENT

If you wish to inject feelings of
brightness and optimism into your life,
surround yourself with colourful
flowers.

Even if such arrangements are not
something you would normally devote
much attention to, flowers have the
power to enhance your mood in
precisely the way nature intended.

DO MORE THAN YOU NEED TO

Effort has a way of bringing its own rewards.

If you work diligently, you not only feel a greater level of satisfaction from what you do, but you achieve much more.

Be satisfied with a job well done. Even if no one notices.

THIS IS YOUR LIFE: STAR IN IT

None of Shakespeare's observations is more profound than 'all the world's a stage, and all the men and women merely players'.

Your time on stage is the interval between birth and death. During this time, you can choose to play any role you choose, and to play it any way you wish.

READ MORE, WATCH LESS

Usually your imagination is more active when you're reading than when you're watching.

This is why literature can have a more uplifting and long-lasting effect than more passive entertainment mediums.

Surround yourself with books and let your imagination work for you.

You miss 100 percent of the shots you never take.

WAYNE GRETZKY

BE OPEN TO THE ANSWER

The events that change the world are often unexpected, maybe even accidents.

While you can plan, you cannot dictate exactly how your world will turn out. You never know what opportunity you could bump into tomorrow, or what great idea might arise during the night.

Be open to everything and your life will be transformed.

ABOUT THE AUTHOR

Paul Wilson is known the world over as the guru of calm.

His first book, *The Calm Technique*, is considered one of the most influential in the genre. His second, *Instant Calm*, was a giant bestseller, translated into twenty languages.

The success continues with *Calm at Work*, *The Little Book of Calm at Work*, *The Little Book of Pleasure* and *The Little Book of Sleep*.

However, the most well-known is *The Little Book of Calm*. With sales of over 3,000,000 it has spent more than three years at the top of the bestseller lists.

Now, with *The Little Book of Hope*, the peace continues to spread.

Feel free to contact the author or share your calm at www.calmcentre.com